W9-ARL-027

Race Against Death

BY SEYMOUR REIT

Illustrated with photos

Cover by Sherry Thompson

SCHOLASTIC INC.
New York Toronto London Auckland Sydney

Photo credits: *UPI:* pp. 4, 8, 20-1 54, 84; *Underwood & Underwood:* pp. 30, 62; *Irwin Nelson:* p. 90.

ISBN 0-590-12124-3

Copyright © 1976 by Seymour Reit. This edition is published by Scholastic Book Services, a division of Scholastic Magazines, Inc., by arrangement with Dodd, Mead and Company.

13 12 11 10 9 8 7 6 5
8
11

Printed in U.S.A.

To Begin

This is a true story. It happened in Alaska, in 1925, to real people — and to real dogs. The places, names, and dates used in this story are accurate. And all the events described are based on real facts.

To make history come to life, the people in it must also come to life. The characters must speak and must feel. Since the events in this book took place many years ago, the author has sometimes had to use his imagination. He has had to "reconstruct" what some people said and thought. But in every case, he has tried to present what these people *might* have said and *could* have felt, as the tense, exciting days unfolded.

Much information for this story came from newspaper and magazine reports and interviews. The author wishes to thank Mr. Richard Brower and his staff at the Microfilm Room of the New York Public Library for making available a great many records of the newspapers and magazines of that period.

For added facts and background material, the author is indebted to the writings of Sally Carrighar, Peter Freuchen, Kenneth A. Ungermann, Elizabeth Ricker, Ralph H. Barbour — and that master storyteller of the Far North, Jack London.

The author also wishes to thank Mr. Frederick A. Allis, of the Explorers' Club of New York City, for making their research library available, and for his kind help and cooperation.

And now, our story...

Seymour Reit
New York, N.Y.

This map shows how the diphtheria serum traveled across Alaska. Starting at Anchorage, it went by rail to Nenana. From there the package was carried by dog sled relays, racing to Nome through the frozen wilderness.

One

January 21, 1925
4:30 P.M.

The huskies had just been fed. Warm and content, they dozed in their long low kennel, safe from the icy wind. But one big black dog was restless. He went to the kennel entrance and pawed the snow. He sniffed the air with a keen nose, testing it nervously.

Balto, like many Alaskan huskies, was descended not only from dogs, but from wolves as well. Deep inside him, wolf ways and dog ways flowed together. Sometimes it was hard to tell where one began and the other ended. Now the wild instincts, bred in his blood, sent a warning signal. Balto growled and twitched his sharp ears. He felt a tenseness in the air; something was going to happen. He didn't know what, but he sensed danger coming. Trouble and danger.

The black hair rose stiffly on the dog's neck. He bunched his great shoulder muscles, eager to meet this new challenge. Then he lifted his muzzle and howled into the wind...

On the other side of town, Dr. Curtis Welch heard Balto howl. But he paid no attention. A howling dog in Nome meant no more than the tooting of a horn on a modern city street. Besides, the doctor had other things on his mind. Near him a young boy lay sick in bed. His face was flushed with fever, and he had trouble breathing.

Mrs. Stanley, the boy's mother, was worried.

"Richard got sick two days ago," she said. "At first I thought it was just a sore throat or a bad cold. But he's been getting worse and worse. So I thought I'd better call you."

Dr. Welch nodded. He felt the boy's pulse, which was very rapid. He examined his bloodshot, half-closed eyes. With a flat wooden stick, he pressed Richard's tongue and looked into his throat. What he saw filled him with concern. There they were — the small white telltale spots. Dr. Welch knew the symptoms well. Six-year-old Richard Stanley had diphtheria.

The doctor turned to Mrs. Stanley and tried to smile. "I'll be back as soon as I pick up some medicine at the hospital," he said, and hurried out.

Nome's hospital, a two-story wooden building, was close by. From a supply cabinet, Dr. Welch took some serum and a hypodermic needle. Then he hurried back to the Stanley house and gave Richard an injection. But he was troubled. The medicine was old. It had been lying in the cabinet for over five years, and could have lost its strength. Besides, Richard was very, very sick. Diphtheria did its work quickly, and it might be too late to save him.

Leaving the Stanleys, Curtis Welch walked slowly back to his own home. The snow crunched under his boots, and his breath came out in clouds of frosty vapor. But he didn't notice the cold. He was deep in thought. And the more he thought, the more he worried.

Just a few days ago, two little Eskimo children

had died. By the time Dr. Welch had been called, it was too late. The children were dying, and he didn't know why. But he felt now that he knew the reason. Most likely, they had died of the same disease Richard Stanley now had.

Diphtheria was a sickness which attacked the throat and lungs. In the Far North, it was a deadly enemy — and the doctor knew it was very contagious. Germs were passed easily, by breathing or coughing. The people of Nome lived close together. There was little to do on long winter nights, so families visited back and forth a great deal. In a town like this, diphtheria would spread like wildfire. Dozens of people could already be infected. And each one would spread the germs still further.

The gray-haired doctor walked down Front Street, as he had done many times before. He passed the Nome Bank and Trust Company. And Howell's law office. And Brown's general store, with a sign in its window advertising dogsled harnesses. The snowy street was empty, and the wooden buildings seemed to lean together for protection against the cold.

Darkness came early here, and the sun had already set. Trudging through the dusk, Curtis

A view of Front Street, the main street of Nome, during the winter of 1925.

Welch worried especially about the Eskimo families.

Alone for years, the Eskimos had lived simple, healthy lives. They were often hungry, but rarely sick. Then the white men came. They brought the Eskimos tools and stoves. And wood for houses. And weapons for hunting. But they brought their diseases, too. The Eskimos had no protection against these strange new diseases, and they easily fell ill.

Dr. Welch remembered the terrible flu epidemic, six years earlier. Whole Eskimo villages had been wiped out. Right here in Nome, even with good medical help, there were many "flu orphans." These were children whose parents had died before the flu epidemic could be stopped.

And now diphtheria was loose — a disease worse than flu. Of course, it could be treated with serum. Diphtheria shots could protect people, and cure the sick ones, if they weren't too ill. Serum was the answer. And this was also the problem. There was a little serum at the hospital, but not nearly enough to stop a bad outbreak of this disease.

Dr. Welch quickened his steps, anxious to get home. He wasn't just worried — he was angry, too. Months ago, he had radioed the U.S. Health Service in Seattle. He had asked them to rush fresh supplies of serum, to have on hand for an emergency. But the precious medicine had never come. And now it was too late.

Nome was icebound in winter. No ship could get through Norton Sound. Dr. Welch knew it would take weeks to send serum all the way from Seattle tc Seward, on Alaska's southern coast. From there it would have to come overland — across miles of ice and snow. A freezing wilderness, with temperatures way below zero. By the time the supplies got through — if they got through at all — hundreds of people would be sick or dying.

Added to all that, he was the only doctor in Nome. Yes, he had excellent nurses — wonderful women like Emily Morgan and Bertha Seville. And there was his dear wife, Lula, who was always a great help. But it would take more than a handful of hard workers to stop a runaway epidemic. It would take serum. Lots of it. Thousands and thousands of units. Without medicine, the whole territory would be in danger.

The doctor stopped at his front door and stamped the thick snow from his boots. From

across town came the sound of a dog howling. It was Balto again. The eerie sound flew high, high into the icy dusk. It hung there for a moment like a strange, mysterious warning.

Inside his heavy coat, Dr. Welch shivered.

The town of Nome was built along the shore of the Bering Sea. In winter — as shown here — the water freezes into mountains of craggy ice, making it impossible for ships to get through.

9

Two

In a cabin near the doctor's house, Jim Anderson brushed frost from the windowpane and peered out. The wind had died down, and it had begun to snow lightly. He walked over to the little iron stove and poured himself a mug of coffee. Then, for the tenth time that morning, he checked his wireless set to make sure everything was in order.

Sgt. James Anderson of the U.S. Army Signal Corps took his job seriously. He and three other

10

soldiers were in charge of Nome's radio station. And radio was the town's lifeline — its main link to the outside world.

Of course, they also had the government mail route. Crack dogsled teams kept a trail open all the way to the railroad station at Nenana. The drivers, called "mushers," worked in relays. They carried mail and packages on wooden sleds pulled by rugged dogs like Balto. Day after day, the teams mushed over the frozen ground, from one outpost to the next. The mail route was very useful — but very slow. A single relay trip from Nenana to Nome took almost a month. And that's why radio was so important. With his wireless set, Sgt. Anderson could contact Fairbanks or Juneau in a matter of minutes. And he could keep in touch with other stations throughout the territory.

Radio was a fairly new invention. Operators sent messages by tapping out a code with a little key. This was called Morse Code. Groups of dots and dashes stood for each letter of the alphabet. At the receiving end, an operator jotted down these dots and dashes as they came through. Then he changed them back into letters and words.

The radio in Nome often clicked busily. But so far, today had been a quiet one. Sgt. Anderson was a little bored. He stretched and looked at his watch. Another hour and he'd be off duty.

The door to the shack suddenly swept open, bringing in a great gust of snow. Anderson recognized a good friend.

"You look frozen," he said with a smile. "Help yourself to coffee, Doc."

Curtis Welch unbuttoned his coat and pulled off his heavy gloves. "Thanks," he said. "I can use some."

The doctor had just come from a meeting at the mayor's office — a meeting he had asked for. The town's leading citizens had all been there. Mr. Summers, manager of the Hammon Mining Company. Mr. Thornton, the Red Cross director. Mr. Rynning, the Superintendent of Schools. And of course, Mayor Maynard.

The worried doctor had told them the bad news. "I'm afraid diphtheria's broken out," he said. "We've had two deaths so far. Another little boy is sick. And I'm sure there are other cases we don't know about yet. We may have an epidemic on our hands."

The faces around the table were grave. They all knew how serious this kind of problem could be.

"How much antitoxin do we have?" someone asked.

Dr. Welch shrugged. "There's a small amount on hand, but it's pretty old. If things get bad, even that won't last more than a few days. Our only hope is to get fresh serum."

Mr. Thornton scratched his chin and frowned. "There's plenty of it back in the States. All we'd ever need. But I don't see how they can get it to us in time."

"Then we'll simply have to find some closer to home," Mayor Maynard said. He turned to the doctor. "Curtis, I authorize you to draft a radio message. Give it top priority. Have our radio people contact Fairbanks, Juneau, and Anchorage. Pass the word along that we must have serum at once. It's an emergency. We'll take anything they can spare."

Dr. Welch nodded. He wondered what would happen if there *wasn't* any serum to be found. But he tried not to think about that.

Now, in the little radio shack, the doctor took a slip of paper from his pocket and handed it to

Sgt. Anderson. "I came straight from the mayor's office," he said. "He wants this to go out immediately. To all stations."

The sergeant read the scribbled message carefully. He and the doctor exchanged a thoughtful look. Then, without a word, Anderson sat down at the wireless set. He put on his earphones and began tapping the key.

Nome calling... Nome calling...

Soon the answer came back.

Go ahead, Nome.... We're standing by...

The sergeant's trained fingers flew up and down, sending the dots and dashes that spelled the call for help. Radio operators, their faces tense, jotted down the words. Then they rushed to deliver their news to the proper officials.

That very night, in spite of all that Dr. Welch and the nurses could do, Richard Stanley died. And others, both children and adults, were beginning to fall ill.

Hour by hour, the epidemic was spreading. But the news was spreading too. In Alaska's cities, doctors hurried to their hospitals, hoping to locate serum. In small outposts along the Yukon River, sled drivers checked their gear, getting ready in case they were needed.

In Nome, Balto, the big black husky, paced restlessly and growled. And in the radio shack, the signals went out, over and over. They crackled through the air, flashing for miles across the frozen tundra, the windswept forests, the ice-covered slopes.

Diphtheria outbreak in Nome...
We need serum badly...
Can you spare any serum?...
Can you help us?...

Three

January 23, 1925
2:00 P.M.

The dogs watched their master come into the yard, his arms loaded with leather gear. They wagged their tails and started yelping. Balto raced over and bumped the man's leg several times with his muzzle.

Leonhard Seppala, the pack's owner, patted Balto's thick coat. "Take it easy, boy. Calm down," he said. "You'll get action soon enough."

Seppala lived in Nome and worked for the Hammon Mining Company. His teams hauled supplies to the company's mine shaft, a few miles from town. They also carried tools and food to smaller mines—called "placer" mines—scattered through the area.

Like everyone else, Seppala was worried about the diphtheria outbreak. And he knew that he and the huskies might soon have a part to play. The old veteran was Alaska's champion sled driver. He had won many races and set many records. People agreed that he was the best driver in the territory, with the fastest, strongest dogs.

Just yesterday, his boss, Mr. Summers, had given him new orders.

"Len," he had said, "while this emergency lasts, I want you to work directly for Mayor Maynard and the doctor. If any serum turns up, you may have to go after it. But it won't be easy. Are you willing to take this on?"

Seppala had smiled. "Of course," he said. "We can do it. The dogs have had a pretty easy winter. I'll start giving them more exercise, to toughen them up. And myself too."

Now, with expert hands, Seppala laid out his gear. He chose certain dogs and began harnessing them to a sled.

Alaskan settlers had learned about dogsleds

from the Eskimos. In the Far North, sleds took the place of trucks and cars. They were perfectly made for the work that had to be done. Most sleds, like the ones Seppala used, were ten or twelve feet long and fairly narrow. Long narrow sleds were easiest to pull through heavy snow.

Dogsleds had light wooden frames and smooth metal runners. The driver stood on a cross-bar at the back. He held two curved handles, which looked like the handles on a plow. These helped him to turn the sled, and to guide it over bumpy ice. Mushing along a trail, a driver sometimes pushed with one foot. If the sled had a heavy load, he would jump off now and then and jog behind it.

Huskies were hitched in pairs—three or more pairs to a sled. But one dog was always hitched alone, in front of the team. This was the lead dog, the smartest and quickest of all. A lead dog had to be keen and alert, ready to obey every order. He had to keep the other huskies in line. He had to know how to follow a trail in any kind of weather. How to sense where the ice was too thin for the sled. Or where a fresh layer of snow was covering a dangerous gap.

The driver commanded the team—but the lead

dog commanded the trail. Men depended on these dogs, and many lives had been saved by their sure instincts.

Leonhard Seppala had two favorite lead dogs, Togo and Scotty. He used one or the other on all his runs. Balto had never served as the leader, but he didn't care. He was a strong, healthy animal and he loved to work. Loafing around the dog yard bored him. But running in harness, following a trail with a clean wind at his back—then he felt really alive.

Now the team was ready to go. Seppala decided to take them along Norton Sound toward Port Safety, then back again. It would be a good hard practice run.

He stepped up on the cross-bar and shouted, "Mush!"

Scotty was in the lead. He and his teammates lunged against their harness straps. The sled began to move. The huskies broke into a trot and the sled glided smoothly over the packed snow.

Balto loped along with his partner. This was work he was made for. His stride was easy. His powerful muscles moved in perfect balance. The black hair rippled across his neck. He sniffed the air with joy.

It was a cold day—about 30 degrees below zero.
But the dogs were protected by their thick shaggy
coats. And running helped to keep them warm.
Seppala was also warmly dressed. He wore thick
mittens. And sealskin Eskimo boots called "muk-
luks." And pants made of reindeer skin. And a
long reindeer jacket with a hood. The hood had a
fringe of wolf's fur. Under the hood, he wore a
woolen cap that covered his ears.

On and on they raced, over the white miles.
The dogs, the sled, the driver flowed smoothly as

Leonhard Seppala and his team, photographed before they left Nome to make contact with the serum relay. Scotty, one of Seppala's lead dogs, can be seen alongside the sled.

one unit. With the others, Balto took the slopes in great easy bounds. At times, Seppala gave an order. When he shouted, "Gee!" Scotty turned to the right. When he shouted "Haw!" Scotty turned to the left. The team mushed along the shoreline for hours, stopping now and then to rest. A few minutes were all the dogs needed.

Then they were ready for the trail again.

It was dark by the time they got back to their own yard. Seppala unharnessed the huskies and fed them. Each dog was given two pounds of dried fish and a lump of seal fat called "tallow."

Balto gulped his food hungrily. Then he curled up in a furry ball with his tail covering his nose. The big dog was drowsy and content. His instincts had already warned him that dangerous work was coming. When it came, he—and the team—would be ready.

Four

January 24, 1925
9:00 A.M.

The *Nome Nugget*, the town's newspaper, carried a special notice on the front page. Because of the epidemic, school would be closed. Parents were told to keep their children home, away from other children. Those who lived in nearby camps and villages were ordered to stay out of Nome until the danger passed. People were advised to wash their hands and faces many times a day.

The newspaper notice tried to sound hopeful. As long as everyone cooperated, it said, there was no cause for worry.

But many people thought otherwise. The disease was slowly spreading. It struck young and old, settlers and Eskimos. First there were a few cases. Then ten. Then twenty. Whenever Dr. Welch's phone rang, the news was the same. Another person had come down with a sore throat and high fever. These were the first signs. Later the dreaded white spots would appear. For many it would be a long illness, then a slow recovery. But some—mostly children—would never get well again.

The doctor decided not to send diphtheria patients to the little hospital, where they might infect others. It was safer to isolate them, and to treat them carefully in their own homes.

Curtis Welch and his nurses worked hard. He put Emily Morgan in full charge of the hospital. This left him free to take care of the diphtheria cases. With Bertha Seville he made endless rounds, giving serum shots to those who were sick or who had been exposed. Lula Welch, also a registered nurse, took over her husband's office routine. She helped the other nurses at the hospital. And she often sat up with a sick child, late into the night.

Meanwhile, in Juneau, Governor Scott Bone

held meetings with his staff. Juneau, the capital of Alaska, was over a thousand miles from Nome. But the radio posts had relayed the news quickly. And the governor had quickly answered. He wired Mayor Maynard that they would do everything possible to find serum—and to send it as soon as they could.

In Washington, D.C., Dan Sutherland went into action. Alaska, in 1925, was not yet a state. And Dan Sutherland was Alaska's "territorial delegate." Working with the U.S. Public Health Service, he alerted all the big drug firms in the country. Factories and warehouses were checked. Serum supplies were traced. Shipping plans were hastily changed. Soon he was able to report back to Juneau. A large supply of antitoxin—over a million units—was ready in Seattle. It would be loaded aboard a ship for the long trip to the port of Seward.

When Governor Bone read Dan Sutherland's message, he shook his head and frowned. "Good —but not good enough," he said. "It may take a month for that shipment to reach Nome. And the epidemic isn't going to wait."

Officials in Washington again contacted Dr. Welch. They offered to gather doctors and nurses from other Alaskan cities and rush them to Nome. But the doctor refused the offer with thanks. He knew the people of Nome. Many, he felt, would be suspicious of outsiders. He and the nurses were trusted, and their orders would be followed. The doctor pointed out that they didn't need extra people—what they needed badly was medicine. The old supply of serum was being used up. In another day or two, it would all be gone.

By now, the rest of the world was beginning to read about the troubled town near the Arctic Circle. People talked about the epidemic in New York and Chicago, in Atlanta and Kansas City. The news spread across the ocean to London and Paris, to Brussels and Rome.

Back in 1900, during the great Gold Rush, the town of Nome had been the largest settlement in the Yukon Territory. Its fame spread everywhere. The small muddy streets were jammed with miners and merchants. And trappers and traders. And shopkeepers and sea captains. And thousands of adventurers, who had rushed north to hunt for precious yellow metal. But now, twenty-five years later, most of the gold was gone. And so were most of the visitors.

Now there were only about 1400 people left—1400 people who waited anxiously for something much more precious than all the gold in Alaska.

Five

January 25, 1925
1:30 P.M.

Dr. Welch was finishing a quick lunch when the telephone rang again. He looked at his wife and sighed. "I'm getting to hate that sound," he said. "All it means is another diphtheria case."

He went into the hall to answer. And when he came back there was a smile on his face—the first smile Lula had seen in many days.

"They've located serum!" he said happily.

The phone call had come from Jim Anderson at the radio shack. There was good news at last. Dr. Beeson, at the Anchorage hospital, had been checking supplies in one of the storerooms, and had found 300,000 units of fresh antitoxin!

Lula, like her husband, was overjoyed. They knew that 300,000 units wasn't a large amount. It took two or three thousand units for just one immunity shot—and a lot more to cure someone already ill. But at least it was something. With careful nursing, and a little luck, it might turn the tide.

When they heard the news in Juneau, Governor Bone and his aides sighed with relief. Dr. Beeson's discovery was the miracle they all needed. Now they had to put the miracle to work. The governor walked over to a large map on the wall of his office. The only railroad in Alaska started at the port of Seward. It went almost straight north through Anchorage, Cantwell, and Nenana, and ended at the city of Fairbanks.

"We can easily move the serum by rail to Nenana," he said to his staff. "The problem is, how do we get it from there to Nome?"

"Why don't we fly it in?" someone asked.

There were a few small planes in Fairbanks.

A typical Eskimo family of the Far North. When the diphtheria epidemic spread through Nome, many families like this were stricken by the disease.

They had been taken apart and stored in a warehouse for the winter. But perhaps one could be assembled quickly. And an experienced pilot might be found to fly it to the isolated town.

The governor hesitated. "Of course, flying is the quickest way—but it's a terrible risk."

Everyone knew what he meant. Airplanes were not yet very dependable. They had never been flown in Alaska during the winter months. Engine oil froze in cold weather, making it dangerous to try a take-off. Violent storms swept through the area. And planes had no radios. It would be very easy to go off course in that snowy world.

And what of the pilot? Early planes had open cockpits. A pilot flying in weather 40 degrees below zero might freeze to death. If the plane got lost, or crashed in a blizzard, the serum would be gone for good. And Nome would be in worse trouble than ever.

Scott Bone knew that time was running out. Every minute counted, and he would have to decide quickly. He wired orders to Fairbanks. The people there were told to get a plane ready, and to have an experienced pilot standing by—if they could find one.

Fairbanks radioed back that they would do their best. But the governor was still undecided. If he ruled against a dangerous plane flight, the only other choice was to use dogsleds. It was a safer way, but a slower one. The mail sleds between Nenana and Nome took almost a month—but those drivers weren't racing against a deadline. They moved at a steady, even pace. And at night they slept in cabins along the way. Traveling in fast relays, never stopping for more than a brief rest, they could save a lot of time.

Someone remembered that Leonhard Seppala had once set a record, mushing the 600-odd miles from Nenana to Nome in only nine days! But the weather had been perfect then. And he had been training his dogs for many weeks before.

"Maybe, with luck, the sleds can make it in ten or twelve days," an aide said.

"I still vote for sending a plane," someone replied.

The debate went on and on. And finally Governor Bone made his decision. "We can't take foolish risks," he said. "This is too important. We're going to use dogsleds."

Most of his aides agreed. Even though it was the twentieth century, some problems still couldn't be solved by machines. People were still the answer. People working together. For years, the settlers of Alaska had trusted in courageous men and strong dogs, and now they would trust in them again.

Juneau wired final instructions to Dr. Beeson at the Anchorage hospital. He was to pack the medicine carefully and put it on board the Alaska Railroad as soon as possible. At Nenana the first sled driver would be waiting—ready to start the long trip overland.

Once more, radios clicked in Signal Corps cabins along the Yukon River. And operators jotted down the coded message.

Request the best musher and team in your section to stand by...ready to receive serum for Nome...starting from Nenana tomorrow...

In the hills around Nome, Leonhard Seppala and his huskies were already preparing. They had been making many practice runs, in case orders should come.

Now, in every village and camp, at every mail post along the way, the word was passed. And people went into action. The best drivers were carefully chosen. The best dogs were collected to make up the fastest teams. Trail routes were checked. Warm clothing was laid out. Harnesses were oiled and sleds were repaired.

The race against time—and death—was beginning.

Six

January 27, 1925
6:00 P.M.

There was a moose on the track. It trotted calmly ahead, completely ignoring the train.

Charlie Mathieson, the engineer, tooted the whistle and grumbled angrily. At this rate, they would never get to Nenana with their precious package. Not that this obstacle was unusual in Alaska. Big animals such as moose and caribou found it hard to wade through the deep snow. It was a lot easier for them to walk along the wooden railroad ties.

Mathieson tooted again and clanged the bell over and over.

"Beat it!" he shouted. "Get your old carcass off the track!"

Bothered by all the noise and fuss, the moose gave up at last. With a toss of its antlers, it climbed onto the snowbank—and the train picked up speed.

The engineer checked his watch and grumbled some more. The 300-mile run from Anchorage was always a slow one. Sometimes the track was blocked by a snowslide. Then men had to go out with shovels and clear the way. Or the rails would ice up. Or a wandering animal like the moose would cause trouble. Most of the time, those things didn't really matter. But today, because of their special cargo, these obstacles mattered a lot.

Hours ago, Dr. Beeson had rushed the serum to the station. He had packed the glass vials carefully, then wrapped the package in a thick blanket. Around this, he had tied some heavy canvas. The final parcel weighed about twenty pounds. Not very big and not very heavy. But what it carried inside would mean life and health to many people.

The doctor worried that the serum might freeze during the trip, and he didn't know whether frozen serum would work. So he wrote out careful instructions. He told the various drivers to warm the package near a stove, whenever they had the chance.

Now the serum was stowed in a corner of the baggage car, under the watchful eye of a conductor. Charlie Mathieson, in the engineer's cab, checked the time again. At the rate they were rolling, they would reach Nenana before midnight. That is, if they didn't run into any more snowslides or bothersome animals. He opened the throttle still more. But he knew he was already getting every bit of speed he could hope for.

The old steam locomotive chugged steadily north. From his window, Mathieson kept a sharp eye on the rails. The miles and hours passed slowly. Palmer...Talkneeta...Summit...Cantwell ...one by one the little towns slid by, silent and cold, as though locked in winter's ice forever. Between the towns, there was nothing but shimmering whiteness. Huge snowbanks loomed on either side of the track. To Charlie Mathieson, they looked like ghost ships riding through the night.

At the Nenana station, the first driver was

waiting impatiently. He was a young mail driver named Bill Shannon. And while he waited, he went over his instructions.

The planners, checking back and forth by phone and radio, had worked it all out. Nenana was the closest point on the railroad. The distance from there to Nome was 670 miles. Along this route, twenty towns had been pinpointed. Some were good sized communities. Others were no more than a handful of tents and cabins.

These towns had unusual names. Some—such as Fish Lake, Ruby, and Whiskey Creek—were reminders of the rough days of the Gold Rush. Other towns—such as Tolovana, Nulato, and Unalakleet—were named after old Indian tribes. At each of these points, a driver and team would be waiting. As soon as the tired driver showed up with the serum, it would be shifted to the waiting sled and tied in place. Then the fresh team and driver would continue racing west.

The trail these men would take wasn't a smooth highway. Or even a simple unpaved road. In some places it was a rough path, worn by the passing of many sleds. In other places it was a set of landmarks—a hill here or a creek there—which the drivers used as guides. And sometimes it was only a "spoor," which the dogs alone could follow. This spoor was the odor left by former teams using the trail.

Bill Shannon, the mail driver, had been picked for the first sled run. His goal was Tolovana, 52 miles away. Waiting for the train, he paced back and forth, beating his arms to keep warm. He knew that time was important, and he was anxious to get on his way.

What he didn't know was that, miles away in Nome, there was a new crisis. That night Dr. Welch used up the last vial of the old serum. Now there was no medicine left, and the town was helpless.

Seven

January 27, 1925
11:00 P.M.

The ice-coated train crawled into the Nenana
station and stopped in a cloud of steam. Shannon
was waiting on the platform. The conductor
climbed from the baggage car and handed him
the package. Also, Dr. Beeson's written instructions.

"Here's the serum" he said. "I sure hope you
fellows make it."

In the locomotive cab, Charlie Mathieson
stretched his aching shoulders, glad that his part

of the job was over. He leaned out of the window and waved to Shannon. Then he tooted the whistle, to signal good luck.

A small group of people had gathered at the station to see the driver on his way. They talked excitedly while he lashed the package on the sled. Shannon shook hands with each of his well-wishers. Then he stepped on the cross-bar, shouted a command, and the team trotted into the night.

Mushing along the trail, heading for Tolovana, Bill Shannon felt a sense of excitement. Ahead of the relay teams lay 670 miles of wilderness. And at the other end was a town waiting to be rescued. The railroad had brought the serum only a small part of the way—the rest would be up to men and dogs.

Shannon's sled skirted along the bank of the frozen Tenana River. He narrowed his eyes. The night was dark, but he could see his huskies outlined against the white snow. He glanced again at the little package, to make sure it was wrapped and tied securely.

The driver stayed alert. In the Far North, men faced all kinds of dangers. Sometimes there were packs of starving wolves to deal with. Or large bears with claws as sharp as razors. There was always a chance of ice breaking, right in front of a racing sled. And sudden storms would roar through the mountain passes like herds of stampeding caribou.

But one danger was greater than all the others. That was the danger of cold. In winter, cold was a bitter enemy that Alaskans had to fight against. And freezing to death was the price if they happened to lose.

Shannon was careful to breathe through his nose. This helped to warm the frigid air. If too much cold air came through his mouth, his lungs could freeze. He was also careful with the huskies. In order to make fast time, he had to keep them moving. But if he ran them too hard, they would start panting heavily. Then cold air would rush in and freeze their lungs too.

As the hours passed, he also watched for signs of limping. Huskies are protected from the cold by thick, shaggy coats—except for one spot. Between a dog's back legs, on the underside, there is very little warm hair. Without cover, this area could become frostbitten. The dog would begin to limp. Next he would become crippled—and he could even die.

On his sled, Shannon carried pieces of rabbit fur. If necessary, he could tie these warm coverings around a dog's haunches. But that would slow the team down, and he didn't want to use the coverings if he could help it.

Shannon watched the trail carefully. Next to cold, his greatest enemy was water. The creeks and streams were frozen over, but water ran under the ice. If the ice suddenly gave way, and a man's—or a dog's—feet got wet, the water would freeze in seconds. The only hope then was to stop and build a fire. Unless the wet areas were thawed out and dried at once, frostbite would set in. Bill Shannon knew men who had lost hands and feet because they didn't act quickly enough.

Now a gray dawn was beginning to spread along the white ridges. Then a feeble sun came up, shedding a frosty light.

The team was running well, and Shannon was grateful for that. He was driving nine dogs—four pairs plus a leader. Sled dogs were dependable and obedient, but their nature was partly wild. Now and then, even in harness, they could get into a mad, snarling scramble. Then the driver had to wade in and restore order. Sometimes a wild rabbit or the scent of a muskrat would excite them. They would bound off on a chase, and had to be pulled back to the trail. But Bill Shannon's dogs seemed to sense the importance of their work, and they gave him no trouble.

A freezing wind began to blow, and Shannon felt his face getting numb. He slapped his cheeks hard with his gloved hands, to start the blood flowing again. He also saw that the dogs' heads were drooping, and he knew it was time for a rest.

"Whoa!" he shouted. He set the brake and the sled stopped. Gratefully, the tired dogs curled up in the snow and flopped their bushy tails over their noses to keep the cold air out. Shannon felt tired, too, as he climbed on the sled. Like the dogs, he turned his back to the wind and bent over very low. He pulled the furry hood close around his face. Resting there, head down, his breath felt warm and comforting. But he reminded himself that he might freeze if he sat there for too long.

After a few minutes, it was time to get moving again. Shannon checked his precious package and roused the dogs. Then he stepped behind the sled and shouted, "Mush!"

The team started off refreshed, following the lead dog as it sniffed out the trail. The sun climbed a little higher in the sky. It seemed to climb very slowly above this cold, unfriendly land.

On and on raced the dogs, the sled's runners hissing over the snow. At noon they came in sight of Tolovana. The huskies, eager for food and rest, put on a last burst of speed. Shannon too was glad the 52-mile trip was over. He and the team had been on the trail for thirteen hours—with only a few brief stops.

When he came wearily into the cabin, Dan Green, the relief driver, greeted him warmly. The tired man carefully placed the package of serum next to the stove to warm it, and then Green brought him a welcome cup of hot soup.

After ten minutes of talk, Green pulled on his heavy parka and picked up the parcel. "I think we should give the serum more time to thaw out," Shannon said. But Dan Green shook his head.

"I can't wait," he said. "We just got another report from Nome. They've had two more deaths. And there are fifteen new diphtheria cases."

Eight

January 28, 1925
6:30 A.M.

In the yard behind his house, Leonhard Seppala began choosing dogs and hitching them to his sled.

The waiting was over at last. He had just gotten a phone call from Mr. Summers. His instructions were to harness a team and start east. Somewhere along the trail—on the other side of Norton Bay—he would meet a relay driver coming with the serum. Seppala was to shift the package to his own sled, then turn around and head right back to Nome.

"We're sure counting on you, Len," Mr. Summers had said. "Good luck!"

Seppala's friend, Gunnar Kaasen, helped him get ready. Kaasen worked for the same mining company as Seppala, and the two men shared the same dogs. Balto, tied to a post near the kennel, watched the preparations eagerly. He sensed, from the way the men spoke, that this was something important.

Seppala explained his plans. On a long run, some dogs could become lame. So he would start off with twenty huskies. Mushing east, he would leave a few at roadhouses and Eskimo huts along the way. Then, on his trip back with the serum, he would have fresh dogs to rely on.

"I'll leave thirteen of the dogs here with you," he said to Kaasen, "in case anything goes wrong."

Gunnar Kaasen nodded. He was a veteran sled racer, and he understood. Seppala had been saved for the toughest part of the trail. On that stretch of wilderness, all kinds of accidents were possible.

Word had spread through town that the champion driver was getting ready to leave. The news cheered everyone up, especially Dr. Welch. "If anyone can get through in this bad weather," he said to Lula, "Seppala can."

Some early risers, bundled against the cold, had come to the yard to wish the driver luck. Seppala decided to take both lead dogs with him. He hitched Togo far out in front, on a long line called a "loose lead." Then came Scotty, in the regular leader's spot. And behind him were the other huskies, harnessed in pairs.

At last all was ready. Seppala shook hands with Kaasen. He waved to the onlookers, who broke into a cheer. Then he stepped up on the sled, shouted, "Mush!" and the team started off.

Balto couldn't believe what was happening. He was being left behind!

A rumble of protest sounded in his throat. He lunged forward, trying to follow the sled. He snapped angrily at the chain attached to his collar. The husky lunged again and again—but the chain held him fast.

Gunnar Kaasen walked over and stroked the dog's black coat. Kaasen had a special fondness for Balto. He had always felt that the big husky had all the makings of a good pack leader.

"Take it easy," he said. "Take it easy, boy."

Balto backed away with a growl, and bared his teeth. He would not be soothed or comforted. The other dogs, also unhappy about being left out, began to bark and yelp. But Balto didn't join them. He stood there tense and rigid, staring after the sled. He watched as Seppala and the team raced smoothly to the top of a ridge, and then disappeared on the far side.

When they were gone, Balto sprawled in the snow with his muzzle resting on his paws. The big dog was confused. He tried hard to grasp what had happened. The trail meant everything to him —nothing else mattered. And now his master had gone on an important journey without him!

Still unbelieving, Balto tried once more to race after the sled. Surely there had been a terrible mistake! With all his strength, he lunged against the maddening chain. But he could not break it.

Finally, the husky gave up. He sat back on his haunches and began to howl. Baying loudly and mournfully over and over, the big black dog cried out his hurt and disappointment.

Nine

Balto, like all huskies, was built for hard work. Now, cheated of it, he sulked unhappily in his yard.

He still felt hurt and confused. He knew nothing of epidemics, or quarantines, or serum shots, of course. But he sensed that something important was going on—and he had been left out. To a trail dog like Balto, this was the worst of punishments. So he sulked in the yard, and wondered where the team had gone.

That afternoon, when Gunnar Kaasen came hurrying through the gate, the unhappy dog hardly glanced at him. But Kaasen was there for a reason. Another meeting had just been held in Mayor Maynard's office. The mayor and his advisers were getting more and more worried. Speed was vital. But the weather was getting worse—and reports had come in that a blizzard was on the way.

"I still have faith in Seppala," Dr. Welch said.

"So do I, Curtis. We all do," the mayor replied. "But this storm might be too much for one man. He'll need help. We *can't* lose the serum now. We can't take chances."

A decision had finally been made. Extra relief drivers would be sent out. They would be placed at three relay points nearest to Nome, ready to carry the package in a final dash.

The men chosen for this job were Charlie Olson, Gunnar Kaasen, and Ed Rohn. Olson was to wait for Seppala at the town of Golovin. Kaasen was to wait at Bluff. And Ed Rohn would stand by at Port Safety. This way, Seppala could be relieved. And precious hours would be saved.

Now, in the dog yard, Kaasen began laying out his sled harness. Balto watched glumly for a minute or two. Then he sat up, beginning to show some interest. What was the man doing? Could it be that another team was getting ready to go out? Half hoping, the husky growled softly and wagged his tail—as though to remind the driver that he was still waiting there.

Gunnar Kaasen walked over, crouched next to Balto, and smiled. He pulled off a mitten and scratched between the dog's sharp ears.

"I always thought," he said softly, "that you would make a great leader, Balto. And now we're going to prove it."

Ten

Across town from Balto's yard, Curtis Welch
sat in his hospital office, feeling weary. He, Lula,
and the nurses had been working steadily. But
there were so many sick, and there was so little
they could do without medicine.

The doctor took a sheet of paper from his desk
and read over the names of the diphtheria vic-
tims. Cameron... Barnett... Lee... Annetoolook
... Englenstadt... Gabriel... He picked up his
pen. At the bottom of the page, he added the

Nome's little hospital, as it looked in 1925. Diphtheria patients were isolated in their own homes, but Dr. Welch used this hospital as a "command post" during the epidemic.

name of the newest patient—Mr. Rynning, the Superintendent of Schools.

This list was getting longer. Now there were five dead, and fifty-two people seriously ill. Another fifty or sixty had been exposed to the germs, and many of those would also get sick. That meant almost one out of every ten people in Nome.

Dr. Welch put the list aside. The diphtheria sufferers weren't just faceless patients—some were his and Lula's closest friends. People they had known for years.

Making the rounds with Bertha Seville, the doctor saw pain and sorrow in many homes. Yet he felt that, so far, they had been fairly lucky. The strict quarantine rules had kept the disease from spreading too fast. But how long would the rules work? Fear—like the epidemic—was growing. Soon it would turn to panic. A few families, hoping to escape illness, had secretly slipped out of town. He knew that others would soon begin running away. And this would only spread the germs further—into places where there was no medical help.

"If that happens," he had said to Bertha, "the whole Yukon Territory will become infected."

Curtis Welch shook his head in despair. They couldn't hold on much longer. Where was Seppala with the serum? What was happening to the relay teams? The drivers had to get through— they *had* to. Without antitoxin, Nome would lose the battle. Every day the terrible disease grew stronger. Every day they came closer to the point where the epidemic would go out of control.

Dr. Welch felt that they were sitting on a time bomb—and that it was getting ready to explode.

Many miles away, the serum race went on. As Leonhard Seppala hurried east, other drivers were mushing west, toward the waiting town. They pushed stubbornly from outpost to outpost, battling the cold. And each tiring run brought the medicine a little nearer.

They mushed hour after hour, night and day. From Kokrines to Ruby, thirty miles...from Ruby to Whiskey Creek, twenty-eight miles ...from Whiskey Creek to Galena, twenty-four miles...from Galena to Bishop Mountain, eighteen miles...from Bishop Mountain to Nulato, thirty miles...

The first half of the trip, along the Yukon River valley, had been the easiest. But now the temperature was dropping, and fierce gales were beginning to blow. The sharp winds made the cold even worse. Here and there, huge snowdrifts blocked the way. Every mile was a challenge, and the teams found the going harder and harder. Now, as each sled reached its relief point, the huskies were limping and the drivers were exhausted.

These drivers were rugged men. Some were native Eskimos. Some were Alaskan Indians. Others were pioneers who had come north to hunt for gold, and decided to stay. Some of their names were: Titus Nikoli, Sam Joseph, Bill McCarty, Harry Pitka, Ed Nollner, and Victor Anagick.

The sled dogs, or huskies, were rugged too. Some were an Eskimo breed called "malamutes." Some were Siberian dogs, bred for running in harness. Others were half wolf—tough and savage. But they all had traits in common. They had broad chests, short necks, and strong legs. They had power and stamina. They could go for days with almost no food and little rest. Huskies never held themselves back. And now they fought through the blinding snow—because it was their work and it had to be done.

*   *   *

All over the United States, people followed the events in Alaska through the newspapers. Every day there were big headlines:

DIPHTHERIA STILL
RAGING IN NOME

DOG TEAMS ON WAY
TO STRICKEN NOME
WITH ANTITOXIN

NOME RELIEF DOGS
REACH HALFWAY POINT

There was also an editorial in *The New York Times*. It told of the country's sympathy for the people of Nome. This terrible epidemic, said the writer, showed the importance of serum in fighting disease. Some older doctors, the editorial went on, didn't believe in using antitoxin. They called it a "new-fangled" idea. But the tragedy in Nome proved, once and for all, that modern medicine held the answer. Diphtheria shots worked. Only serum could stop the epidemic.

All over America, in their warm, comfortable homes, people read about the serum race. They followed the news stories flashed from Alaska by radio—stories of courage and suspense.

But words printed in a newspaper couldn't tell everything. Words in a paper couldn't really explain the suffering of the sled drivers, or the weariness of a hard-working doctor. Or the panic that was slowly creeping through Nome.

Eleven

January 31, 1925
5:30 P.M.

The men almost missed each other in the blinding, swirling snow. But just in time, Leonhard Seppala saw the other sled coming toward him. It was the sled carrying the serum west.

Hank Ivanoff, the relay driver, greeted Seppala with a wave of his hand. The wind was howling so loudly it was hard for the men to talk. They shifted the package of serum to Seppala's sled. Ivanoff also gave Seppala the tattered paper with Dr. Beeson's instructions. Then, with a nod, a quick handshake, a pat on the shoulder, the two drivers parted company.

Now it was time for the tough run back to Nome. Seppala swung his sled around and shouted at the dogs. Their first goal was the town of Golovin, 91 miles away. So far, the serum had traveled 500 miles from the rail station at Nenana. But it still had 170 miles to go—and these would be the hardest.

Seppala's dog, Scotty, had been left at a relay point, and Togo was now in the lead. Togo was a Siberian husky. He was small for a sled dog, but a born pack leader. Seppala felt—and many drivers agreed—that Togo was just about the smartest dog in all of Alaska. He also had a special talent. No matter what the trail was like, whether smooth or hilly, Togo was able to travel in a perfectly straight line. He never went off his course—and this saved the team a great deal of time and energy.

Led by the tough little Siberian, the dogs pushed into the teeth of the storm. Togo yelped to his mates, spurring them on. Seppala squinted through the dusk. The Arctic wind whipped ice and snow into his eyes, making it hard for him to see.

This photograph, taken after the serum race, shows Leonhard Seppala with Togo, one of his favorite dogs. Togo led the team on a grueling 91-mile run, from Shaktolik to Golovin.

Before long, they came to the edge of Norton Bay—and now Seppala had to make an important choice. The safest plan was to stay on solid ground, and to circle all the way around the bay. But this would add many hours to the trip. The bay was frozen, and they could take a shortcut straight across the ice. But it was a dangerous route. In this kind of gale, the ice could begin to crumble and crack. On their way across, the sled might be trapped. If the ice broke, they could easily freeze or drown. And, of course, the serum would be lost.

Standing on the bank in the howling wind, Seppala thought of his own family back in Nome. He thought of Dr. Welch and the brave nurses, and all the others who were working hard and waiting anxiously. Waiting for a certain package that meant so much to all of them.

"We're sure counting on you, Len," Mr. Summers had said....

The veteran made his decision. He would trust in Togo's instincts—and his own experience. He would save time and take the shortcut. Seppala shouted to the team. Without a second's pause, the faithful Togo started across the ice.

Now the wind came thundering with the force

of a locomotive. There were no guide points for Togo to follow. He had to find his way by using his nose—and his uncanny sense of direction. As they mushed along, Seppala kept his eyes on the ice just ahead. He listened for sounds of cracking. He watched for "ice spears." These were broken chunks of ice, sometimes pushed by the water churning underneath. The chunks were as sharp as razors, and could slash a dog's feet badly. On his sled, Seppala had small flannel coverings which he could tie around their paws, if he had to. Anxiously, he watched the route which Togo was taking.

In most spots, the ice was rough. But here and there, it became as smooth as glass. On one of these smooth glassy patches, a sudden gust blew the sled sideways. The dogs slipped, lost their balance, and tumbled over. There was a mad scramble. Seppala lost valuable time untangling the harness and getting the team started again. Then they went on, moving quickly but carefully.

It took several hours for the huskies to work their way across the frozen bay—but to the tired driver it seemed more like weeks. In the darkness, they climbed up at last on the far bank. They had made it safely.

Once on solid ground, Seppala headed for shelter in a nearby Eskimo hut. He moved the dogs into a shed and fed them some dried fish. Then he carried the serum into the hut, where his Eskimo friend had a fire going in the stove. Carefully, Seppala put the package near the stove. Then he fell on a cot, exhausted.

After an hour's rest, he decided to go on again. The old Eskimo warned him to wait. Outside, the storm was building into a full-scale blizzard. But Seppala shook his head. Saving time was all that mattered now.

"Golovin..." he mumbled wearily, "got to reach Golovin..."

Soon after the team started off, the storm grew more violent. Seppala could barely see more than a few yards in front of the sled. He noticed that the dogs were beginning to stiffen up. This was a danger sign. He stopped the sled and massaged their frozen limbs. Then he brushed away the coating of ice that had formed on their muzzles.

Once more the team pushed forward, numb with cold. Seppala kept shouting words of encouragement. Not just to keep up the dogs' spirits, but his own as well. They struggled on through the blackness, trapped in an icy, howling whirlwind. Finally, Seppala saw lights up ahead, and knew that they had made it to Golovin.

The old veteran was relieved. Then he began to worry. This was one of the worst blizzards he had ever known. And he felt completely worn out. Even with fresh dogs, he wondered how he could go all the way to Nome. Staggering into the town, Seppala didn't know that there had been a change of plan. He didn't know about Kaasen and Balto. Or that Charlie Olson was waiting right there at Golovin with fresh, well-rested dogs —ready to continue the race.

For Leonhard Seppala, Togo, and the other valiant huskies, the ordeal was over. Their trip through the storm had been the longest run of any relay team. Now, thanks to them, the serum was closer to Nome than ever.

But there was still a long way to go, and the storm was getting worse every minute.

Twelve

February 1, 1925
8:00 P.M.

Sgt. Anderson pulled off his earphones and turned to Dr. Welch, who was sitting near him in the radio shack. Anderson looked worried.

"There's a lot of static, but I got through to Bluff," he said. "It sounds bad, Doc. They're right in the middle of a rip-roaring blizzard. The winds are up to fifty miles an hour."

Curtis Welch stood up and shook his head wearily. He walked over to the window and looked out at the storm. Fifty-mile winds—why, that was hurricane force! He thought of the drivers and dog teams, out there somewhere in the blinding gale. And suddenly he felt very helpless.

At that moment, fifty miles away, another man was staring out the window. Gunnar Kaasen, in the mail cabin at Bluff, watched the snow. He could see only a few yards into the darkness. The thermometer, hanging outside, showed 30 degrees below zero. Well, that was cold—but he'd known it a lot colder. The wind was another matter. The wind really worried him.

Kaasen and the dogs had made their run from Nome without too much trouble. He had taken all thirteen dogs with him—six pairs, plus Balto. He had just given them an extra meal of seal tallow, for warmth and energy. And now they were resting in the big kennel next to the cabin.

Gunnar Kaasen began pacing up and down. Anxious thoughts crept through his mind. All he could do now was to wait—and worry. Had Seppala made it into Golovin? Could Charlie Olson get through this blizzard? Olson's run was fairly short—but it could be very rough in this kind of weather. He might have had a bad accident. Right now, he might be lying somewhere on the trail, freezing to death.

Kaasen paced back and forth, back and forth, over the rough wooden floor. And the more he paced, the more tense he became.

Suddenly the huskies began to yelp and bark. Kaasen ran to the door and threw it open. He could just make out a sled crawling through the darkness. It stopped outside the cabin. Charlie Olson staggered in, his face coated with ice. The driver almost fell, and Kaasen had to help him into a chair.

"The serum..." he gasped. "Get...package...Take care of dogs..."

Kaasen pulled on his gloves and his sealskin coat, and hurried out. He unhitched the dogs and moved them into the kennel, which was big enough to hold both teams. Then he untied the parcel, carried it inside, and put it near the stove.

Olson was exhausted. Kaasen gave him some hot coffee. Little by little, the driver's strength came back. And soon he was able to talk.

"It's a lucky thing they sent us out, Gunnar," he said. "Seppala just barely made it. He was all played out. His dogs were so tired, they fell right over·in their harness. I never saw anything like it."

Olson held his hands toward the warm stove. "I

had a rough time, too," he went on. "The gale blew my sled off the trail four or five times. Knocked it clean over."

The driver studied his fingers. They were a dead, ashy white.

"I took my gloves off to put blankets around the dogs," he explained. "My hands got frozen. I may lose a couple of fingers."

Kaasen examined Olson's hands with an expert eye.

"No, Charlie—I think you'll be all right," he said, "but you'll have a lot of pain when your circulation starts coming back."

Olson shrugged. He didn't mind the pain. He didn't even mind losing a few fingers. Like the other relay drivers, his thoughts had become locked on a single idea. Nothing mattered any more, except getting the serum to Nome.

In a little while, Kaasen checked his watch. Then he put on his heavy parka again.

"I'll get started," he said. "It's now or never."

Charlie Olson nodded. "Right, Gunnar. The storm won't get any better, that's for sure."

Kaasen's goal was Port Safety, the town nearest to Nome. While Olson watched from the doorway, Kaasen quickly lashed the package on the sled. Then he collected his dogs and hitched them in place. He had to take off his gloves to handle the harness buckles—and noticed that, in just a few minutes, his fingers began to get numb.

When all was ready, he turned and waved good-bye to Olson. Then he walked to the head of the waiting team. He crouched next to Balto and silently stroked the dog's head. The husky lifted his muzzle and wagged his bushy tail. Between man and dog there seemed to be a special bond— a secret understanding that went beyond speech or gesture.

After a moment, Kaasen stood up. He trotted to the rear of the sled and stepped on the cross-bar.

"Mush!" he shouted. "Pull, Balto!"

The husky lunged against his straps and the sled began to move. As the dogs started, Kaasen kept shouting, trying to urge them on. But the mocking wind swept his words away into the frozen blackness.

Thirteen

February 1, 1925
10:30 P.M.

Head down...nose to the ground...find the spoor...ears sharp and alert...listen for commands...keep the team working...bark and growl to spur on the slackers...

Balto the leader plowed through the storm, feeling a surge of power. The ruff stood up on his strong neck. His muscles rippled smoothly, meeting every demand made on them. Ice dust, sharp as a thousand needles, stung his face. He narrowed his eyes to protect them—but he studied the trail as keenly as ever.

By instinct, his mind reached out in two directions. He was aware of the trail ahead, with all its dangers. He was also aware of the driver on the cross-bar, who had to be obeyed.

Soon a heavy snowdrift blocked their way. Balto tried to push through. But the snow was thick and deep, and the dogs floundered up to their chests. Gunnar Kaasen tugged on the sled handles and backed the team out. Then he shouted "Gee!" and Balto swerved to the right. Slowly, painfully, the team worked its way around the drift. In a few minutes, Kaasen shouted "Haw!" and Balto swung quickly to the left. He moved on, testing the ground until he found the trail again.

This happened time after time during the long night. Each time they circled a drift, or skirted a patch of weak ice, Balto brought them back to the right place. Gunnar Kaasen smiled with satisfaction—Balto was proving himself.

As the miles passed, Kaasen felt the cold spreading under his clothes. He hopped off the bar and jogged behind the sled. It made his blood flow fast, and he felt warmer. But it only lasted a moment. Like the other relay drivers, he wore many layers of clothing. And for a good reason. The heat from his body stayed trapped in these layers, giving him a cushion of warmth. But when a fierce wind blew, it went right through the layers. It blew away his cushion of body heat, and there was nothing to stop the cold. This was known in the Far North as "wind chill."

Now Kaasen felt the chill creeping across his skin. It seemed to crawl into his chest, his stomach, his muscles—into his very bones. He tried running again. He shook his hands, and moved his stiff fingers in their sealskin gloves. He slapped his cheeks, which were beginning to feel numb.

The sled crept through the darkness, and the storm closed in. Soon Kaasen could only see as far as his wheel dogs. These were the two dogs nearest to the sled. Kaasen knew that, somewhere in front, Balto was leading them faithfully. But the driver no longer had any control. He was cut off in a wild gray nightmare. The sled handles were his only contact with reality—and he gripped them tightly.

Balto threw a quick look over his shoulder. He, too, felt alone. All he could see now were the two dogs directly behind him. Everything else was lost in the whirlwind. The husky yelped loudly, to reassure the others. Then he pushed on.

Head down...nose to the ground...find the scent...stay alert...keep the team moving... whatever happens, follow the trail...

The sled bumped and tilted. Kaasen knew that they were moving up a steep hill. As they struggled upward, he kept breathing through his nose. His chest felt ready to burst, and he longed to open his mouth wide and take in great gulps of air. But he knew that it would mean frozen lungs —then death.

It seemed like days before the sled crested the hill and started down the far side. The tired dogs half slid through the thick, powdery snow. At the bottom, Kaasen set his brake and the team rested. But in this kind of storm, even resting was an effort.

Ten minutes later, they were moving again. They mushed for miles through heavy woods, and reached a snow-covered plain. In summer, this was a swampy marshland, but now it was frozen solid. On the open plain, the Arctic wind went mad. An angry gust lifted the sled and the dogs, and flung them aside. The team fell in a wild tangle of harness. Kaasen tumbled head over heels, as though slapped by a huge invisible hand.

With a groan, the driver pulled himself to his feet. He staggered over to the dogs and began to untangle their gear. When he straightened up the sled, he glanced into it—and his heart almost stopped beating.

The package of serum wasn't there!

The weary man couldn't believe his eyes. He realized, with a sick feeling, that he had tied it hurriedly, back at Bluff. The ropes must have worked loose. And, as the sled bounced over the trail, the package had fallen out!

But *where* did it happen? Did he lose it hours ago? Or just now, when the sled was blown over?

In a panic, Kaasen threw himself into the snow. It was too dark to see well, so he groped blindly, his heart pounding. He had to find the serum! He couldn't lose it now—not when they were so close to their goal!

Balto and the other huskies stood by obediently, while Kaasen floundered in the drifts, feeling with his gloved hands.

"Let me find it," he whispered. "Please let me find it!"

Kaasen fought against terror. The serum *had* to be here, somewhere! Half sobbing, he crawled round and round, going in wider circles. Snow whipped into his face. Splinters of ice cut through his gloves and slashed at his knees, but he felt nothing. Nothing but a deadly, creeping fear.

Suddenly his leg bumped against a hard surface. He pounced on the object and brushed away the snow. Then relief swept over him, and he breathed a prayer of thanks. He had found the package, safe in its canvas cover.

This time, Kaasen tied the serum tightly on the sled. He wouldn't make the same mistake again. Ready at last, he took his place and gave the signal. Balto could just barely hear him above the wind. He barked, and the team lunged forward.

Head down... nose to the ground... track the scent... hold the trail... keep the lead line straight and taut...

Suddenly there was danger! Balto reared back and stood still, his legs rigid. The dogs piled up behind him, and began yelping in confusion. Kaasen was puzzled. Why did Balto stop? He set the brake and stumbled forward to investigate.

One quick look gave him the answer. A racing creek had broken through its covering of ice. Freezing water was gushing out, just inches away from Balto's feet. If the dog hadn't stopped short, the team would have floundered into it. And Kaasen would have lost much time getting their paws dried out again.

The driver smiled and patted Balto gratefully. He inched the team carefully to one side. They mushed upstream, and made a safe crossing where the ice was still solid. Then once more they worked back to the trail. Numbly they kept going, putting one foot in front of the other.

As the sled neared Port Safety, the storm began to ease. The gale died down enough so Kaasen could see for a short distance. With relief, he picked out some familiar landmarks. Yes, Port Safety was just ahead.

Kaasen saw his goal—a small mail cabin perched on a hillside. And now he became confused. There were no lights showing in the cabin. The whole cluster of buildings was dark and quiet. And he heard no dogs barking.

The driver's mind raced with unanswered questions. Wasn't Ed Rohn supposed to be here, ready to relieve him? Had there been another change of plans? Was there some misunderstanding?

Half-frozen, Kaasen forced himself to think calmly, clearly. Maybe Ed Rohn was in the cabin, still asleep. If so, it would take time to wake him up. Time for him to get dressed, and harness his dogs. And valuable minutes would be lost. Rohn was a good racing driver, he knew. But the man and his team had no experience mushing through a bad storm. It would be risky for them. They might not be able to make it.

Kaasen's brain was spinning. Should he go find out what was wrong? But that would take a while. He looked at Balto and the other huskies. They were tired, but still running well. The storm had eased up, and Nome was only 20 miles away...

The mail cabin loomed above them on the hillside, dark and still. It seemed to send a wordless message. And Gunnar Kaasen suddenly made up his mind. There was no time to waste. Not a minute, not a second. He turned to his team and snapped the harness lines.

"Mush!" he shouted. "We're going to Nome!"

At first, the sled moved smoothly. The air

cleared, and the huskies made good time. Then, a few miles outside of Port Safety, the blizzard thundered in again. The wind howled and the snow whirled around them. Ice dust slashed at Kaasen. Time after time, he had to brush a thick crust of frost from his bleeding face. Then Kaasen noticed, with a shock, that he could no longer see his wheel dogs. The snow was so heavy he couldn't see past the end of his sled.

"Now it's up to you, Balto," he muttered through cracked, frozen lips.

Out in front, the big dog clung to the trail. The wind made it very hard to follow the spoor. Muzzle close to the ground, eyes half-closed, he fought with all his instincts. By now, Balto was limping. Splinters of ice were cutting painfully into his paws. He could tell, by the feel of the traces, that the other dogs were limping, too. But, pain or no pain, he didn't falter or slow the pace.

Another mile passed slowly. And another. And the gale raged with new fury. To Kaasen, it seemed as if the storm felt cheated. For hundreds of miles it had lashed at the relay teams, trying to destroy them. But the race had gone on. And now, with only a few miles left, the storm was making one last deadly try.

Weary, anxious, half-dead with cold, Gunnar Kaasen looked up at the thick, murky sky.

"We're not licked!" he shouted hoarsely. "We're going...to Nome! We're...going to make it!"

Balto heard his master raving at the wind. He didn't understand the words, but he sensed their meaning. A low growl rumbled deep in his throat —and he matched Kaasen's anger with a savage defiance of his own.

Head down, shoulders hunched, blind to the cold and the pain, Balto limped forward....

Fourteen

February 2, 1925
5:00 A.M.

Thump...thump...thump...
Dr. Welch sat up in bed. He listened, puzzled.
Who was pounding on their front door at this
strange hour? Or had he been dreaming?
Thump...thump...
There it was again. Yes, there *was* somebody at
the door. Careful not to wake Lula, he climbed
out of bed, pulled on his bathrobe, and went un-
happily downstairs. More trouble, he thought.
Probably a neighbor, reporting a new diphtheria

case. Or even another death. Maybe something had gone wrong with the serum relay, and they were coming to break the news.

The doctor opened the front door. Something staggered in and half fell against him. Startled, Dr. Welch drew back. The figure looked like a weird snow-covered monster—a creature straight from the North Pole. Then he recognized the face under its mask of ice.

"Kaasen!" he shouted. Quickly, he helped the driver into a chair. He threw back Kaasen's hood, felt his pulse, and examined his glazed eyes.

"You'll be all right, Gunnar," he said. "Sit here quietly. You're just totally exhausted." Then he asked an important question—but dreaded to hear the answer.

"What happened to the serum?"

Kaasen raised a weary arm and gestured toward the door.

"Serum..." he mumbled, "outside...on sled."

Dr. Welch broke into a grin and patted Kaasen's shoulder.

"You did it!" he said. "You did the impossible!"

He pulled a coat over his bathrobe, shoved bare feet into his boots, and hurried out. The storm

Gunnar Kaasen poses here with his famous lead dog, Balto. It was Balto who led Kaasen's team through a raging blizzard, on the final race to Nome.

had eased once again, and dawn was beginning to spread on the horizon. The doctor untied the canvas package and carried it into the house. It was the most beautiful thing, he decided, that he had ever seen.

"Lula!" he shouted excitedly. "Lula, wake up! The serum is here!"

Lula Welch, in robe and slippers, came bustling downstairs. She ran to Kaasen and hugged him happily, even though the driver still wore his icy clothing.

"You take off those things and try to rest," she said. "I'll make you something hot to drink."

She hurried into the kitchen where her husband was already opening the package near the stove. He examined the vials of serum. As he expected, all of them were frozen solid. But the doctor wasn't worried. He had already checked with Seattle, and the Public Health people had reassured him. If the serum was handled with care, they radioed, it wouldn't be harmed. Once thawed, it would work as well as ever.

Dr. Welch ran to the phone. He called Emily Morgan at the hospital, waking her up with the good news. Then he spoke to Bertha Seville and quickly outlined his plans. As soon as the serum thawed, he would rush it to the hospital. They would arrange for other nurses to help out. Then they would get to work.

"We're going to have a busy few days," he said to her, "but thank heavens we have the medicine. I've got a feeling everything will be all right, now."

When Dr. Welch hung up, he noticed Lula studying a calendar hanging on the wall. She shook her head in wonder.

"Curtis," she said, "I was just checking the dates. Do you know what those men did? They made that whole trip from Nenana, blizzard and all, in *five and a half days!*"

Curtis Welch smiled. Suddenly the gray, cold morning seemed crowded with miracles. Then he remembered something else.

"Kaasen," he said. "He needs looking after."

The doctor hurried into the other room. To his surprise, Kaasen wasn't there. And the front door was standing open. Dr. Welch was curious. Still wearing his coat and boots, he went out into the snowy street. Then he stopped and watched quietly.

Gunnar Kaasen was bending over the team, which was still hitched to the sled. He was trying somehow to embrace all the dogs at once. Then the driver stumbled over to the lead dog and dropped to his knees. He hugged and stroked the big husky.

"Balto..." he whispered, "Balto..."

Kaasen lifted one of the dog's bleeding paws. With tears rolling down his face, he began pulling out the sharp splinters of ice.

"Balto...Balto..." the driver repeated, over and over again.

The big dog, head drooping, wagged his tail slowly. He felt tired—more tired than he had ever felt before. But something stirred inside him—a strong new feeling, blended of pride and deep contentment.

Balto's instincts told him that they had succeeded. Whatever it was these men wanted, the sled dogs had helped to achieve it. They had beaten an Arctic blizzard. They had finished their work.

Now the struggle was over, and the team had come home.

What Happened After

Just as Dr. Welch had hoped, the fresh supply of serum helped to turn the tide. After it was put to use, there were no more diphtheria deaths. And the epidemic was soon brought under control.

A few weeks later, the larger serum shipment, sent from Seattle on the *S. S. Alameda*, also reached Nome. And on February 21st, exactly one month after the first diphtheria case, the quarantine was ended.

Diphtheria, at that time, was a serious problem. Every year in America over 200,000 people fell sick, and there were about 20,000 diphtheria deaths. Today, thanks to improved antitoxin, the disease is no longer a menace. Like polio and smallpox, it can now be safely controlled with immunity shots.

For a little while after the serum race, Dr. Welch, his helpers, the drivers, and the sled dogs were all treated as heroes. People talked admiringly of Kaasen and Seppala, of Togo and Balto. And there were many stories written about their race through the blizzard.

One sad story appeared in *The New York Times* saying that Balto's lungs had frozen, and that the great dog had died. But this proved to be an error. Balto and some other dogs did suffer injuries, but after a while they recovered well.

In August of 1925, the United States Government awarded medals to the relay drivers. Gunnar Kaasen, Leonhard Seppala, Charlie Olson, Bill Shannon, Hank Ivanoff, and all the others were honored for their heroic work.

Soon after that, the country turned to new matters and the story of Nome was almost forgotten. Almost, but not quite...

If you happen to live in New York City—or go there on a visit—take a trip to Central Park.

This bronze statue of Balto, created by Frederick G. Roth, was placed in New York's Central Park after the serum race. It honors not only Balto, but all the brave huskies who took part in the incredible rescue.

Walk into the entrance on 67th Street and Fifth Avenue. Follow a pleasant winding path, past a sloping lawn and a children's playground.

After a hundred yards or so, you will come to a large granite rock. On top of this rock is the statue of an Alaskan husky. The dog's bronze back has been rubbed shiny by the hundreds of children who, over the years, have climbed up on it. This statue was placed in the park by a group of grateful citizens. It is a model of Balto, and his name appears on the plaque below. But the beautiful statue is really a tribute to all the sled dogs —to Togo, Scotty, Jack, Dixie, Buck, and all the teams who worked so hard to save a town in danger.

If you squint your eyes as you look, the big bronze husky seems to almost come alive. He stands there, eyes and ears alert, gazing north— as if he were hoping to see the ridges and valleys of far-off Nome.

Today, Nome is no longer isolated. There are many airfields in Alaska. Hundreds of "bush planes" buzz through the skies, keeping in touch with every community and village. But dogsleds are still important in the Far North. They are still used in many places, and the cry of "Mush!" can often be heard on the icy white trails.

Now and then, an old-timer may stop to watch one of these teams gliding along the horizon. As he watches, he may be reminded of other times, and other teams.

With a smile, he may even remember what once happened to a little town on the Bering Sea, many years ago.